HE CHOSE
THE
NAILS

HE CHOSE
THE
NAILS

WHAT GOD DID TO WIN YOUR HEART

STUDY GUIDE
GROUPS / INDIVIDUALS
FIVE SESSIONS

MAX LUCADO

WITH CHRISTINE M. ANDERSON

THOMAS NELSON
Since 1798

Contents

How to Use This Guide

GROUP SIZE

The *He Chose the Nails* video study is designed to be experienced in a group setting such as a Bible study, Sunday school class, or any small group gathering. To ensure everyone has enough time to participate in discussions, it is recommended that large groups break up into smaller groups of four to six people each.

MATERIALS NEEDED

Each participant should have his or her own study guide, which includes notes for video segments, directions for activities and discussion questions, as well as practices to deepen learning between sessions.

TIMING

The time notations—for example (14 minutes)—indicate the *actual* time of video segments and the *suggested* times for each activity or discussion. Adhering to the suggested times will enable you to complete each session in about an hour. If you have a longer meeting, you may wish to allow more time for discussion and activities.

PRACTICE

Each session includes an application activity called a practice for group members to complete on their own between meetings. Although the practice is completed outside of group time, it's a good idea to briefly review it before concluding the meeting to clarify any questions and to make sure everyone is on board.

FACILITATION

Each group should appoint a facilitator who is responsible for starting the video and for keeping track of time during discussions and activities. Facilitators may also read questions aloud and monitor discussions, prompting participants to respond and ensuring that everyone has the opportunity to participate.

OPTIONAL SESSION FOR WEEK 6 OF LENT

An optional session has been provided for small groups using this study as part of a churchwide campaign for Lent. During this final session, the participants will not watch a video but will have an extended time of Bible study and discussion as they prepare to celebrate Easter.

SESSION 1

He Chose to Be One of Us

God did what the law could not do. He
sent his own Son in a body like the bodies
we sinners have. And in that body God
declared an end to sin's control over us by
giving his Son as a sacrifice for our sins.

Romans 8:3 NLT

You alone are the God for us—because you
alone are the God who has been one of us. You
felt what we feel, you touched the death that
we know, you came to us as Immanuel:
God with us.

Ann Voskamp, aholyexperience.com

WELCOME

Welcome to session 1 of *He Chose the Nails*. If this is your first time together as a group, take a moment to introduce yourselves to one another before watching the video. Then let's begin!

VIDEO: *HE CHOSE TO BE ONE OF US* (14 MINUTES)

Play the video segment for session 1. As you watch, use the outline provided to follow along or to take additional notes on anything that stands out to you.

Notes

The gifts of Easter are the most precious gifts any person could ever receive because they cost God so much to give.

God's greatest gift of all—his greatest act of love for us—was sending Jesus into our world.

Jesus gave up:

Timelessness: Jesus swapped eternity for calendars. The Bible tells us God is "beyond our understanding! The number of his years is past finding out" (Job 36:26). There is no moment when God was not God, for he is eternal.

Boundlessness: Jesus gave up being a spirit to live in a body. One moment he was a boundless spirit; the next moment he was flesh and bones.

Sinlessness: Jesus became sin for us. An object that symbolizes the consequences of sin in humanity's heart is a thornbush (see Genesis 3:17–18; Numbers 33:55; Proverbs 22:5; Matthew 7:16). The thorny crown on Christ's brow is a picture of the fruit of our sin that pierced his heart.

We are "by nature children of wrath" (Ephesians 2:3 NASB). Though we have been made in God's image, we're corrupt at the core. The sinless One took on the face of a sinner so that we sinners could take on the face of a saint.

Jesus never knew the fruits of sin until he became sin for us (see 2 Corinthians 5:21). When he was crucified, he cried out in a loud voice, "My God, my God, why have you forsaken me?" (Matthew 27:46). Those are not the words of a saint but the cry of a sinner.

The crown of thorns could have been made—and should have been worn—by every one of us. But it was not, thanks to the greatest gift of all.

Why did God give us this gift? "For God so loved the world that he gave his one and only Son, that whoever believes in him shall not perish but have eternal life" (John 3:16).

God did it for us—just for us—because he loves us.

GROUP DISCUSSION (44 MINUTES)

Take a few minutes to talk about what you just watched.

1. What part of the teaching had the most impact on you?

Receiving the Gifts of Easter

2. Imagine for a moment that you have decided to do a random act of kindness for a stranger by leaving a $100 bill in a public place (such as a park, a lobby, or a store aisle). After placing the cash where it can be easily spotted, you hide nearby to see who will find it. As you wait, you begin to think about who might receive your gift.

   • What kind of person do you most hope *will* and *will not* find your gift? For instance, you might hope a struggling single parent *will* find it, and that a compulsive gambler *will not* find it. Identify three or four kinds of people you would consider *deserving* recipients and three or four you would consider *less than deserving*.

   • If someone in the less-than-deserving category were to find your gift, what thoughts might you zing his or her way? For example, *You don't deserve it. You'd better not waste it. Someone else needs it more.*

- The same way we think about giving gifts is often reflected in the way we think about receiving them. Consider the internal response you tend to have when you are the recipient of a gift, whether material or immaterial. What might the thought zingers you just identified suggest about your own ability to receive a gift, perhaps especially when it is unexpected? Do you send similar thought zingers to yourself? (*I don't deserve it; I better not waste it; someone else needs it more.*) What other internal dynamics sometimes make it difficult for you to truly receive a gift?

3. Max described the period leading up to Easter as a season of gifts—precious gifts that God gave us at the cross, such as the crown of thorns. For centuries, Christians throughout the world have used the season of Lent to prepare themselves spiritually so that nothing prevents them from receiving and celebrating the greatest Easter gift of all—the resurrected Christ.

   The word *Lent* comes from the Old English word *lencten,* which means *spring.* In its earliest observance, Lent was a time for new converts to prepare for their baptism on Easter Sunday. Today, Lent marks the forty-day period before Easter that begins each year on Ash Wednesday.* Although it is traditionally a time devoted to self-examination, self-denial, and repentance, Lent sinks its deepest roots into the joyful expectation of new life through God's forgiveness and steadfast love. This sense of Lent is evident in the words of Jesus: "The kingdom of God has come near. Repent and believe the good news!" (Mark 1:15). We also find it in this passage written by the prophet Joel, traditionally read at the beginning of Lent:

> "Even now," declares the LORD, "return to me with all your heart, with fasting and weeping and mourning." Rend your heart and not your garments. Return to the LORD your God, for he is gracious and compassionate, slow to anger and abounding in love, and he relents from sending calamity (Joel 2:12–13).

The time during which Joel was a prophet was one of great prosperity. God had richly blessed his people, but their hearts had grown cold over time. They began to take "God and his blessings for granted. [Their] faith had degenerated into an empty formalism and their lives into moral decadence."[1] Through the prophet, God pleaded with his people to return to him with their whole heart.

The season of Lent issues a similar call to God's people today. It is a time to take seriously the areas of our lives in

---

* There are actually forty-six days between Ash Wednesday and Easter, but the six Sundays in Lent are traditionally set aside as days of renewal (considered "mini-Easters") and so are not counted as part of Lent.

which we fall short, feel defeated, or have grown cold. And we
do so not to beat ourselves up but to prepare for God's gifts:

> Lent is a time for discipline, for confession, for honesty,
> not because God is mean or fault-finding or finger-
> pointing but because he wants us to know the joy of
> being cleaned out, ready for all the good things he now
> has in store.[2]

This process of being cleaned out is part of how we
return to God with all our heart, which is what Lent is meant
to help us do.

- How would you describe your understanding and experience of Lent over the years? In what ways is it similar to
  or different from the description you just read?

- What, if anything, shifts in your perspective when you
  think of Lent less as a season of guilt or giving something
  up and more as a time to be intentional about preparing
  to receive joy and good things from God?

- The Hebrew verbs translated *rend* and *return* in Joel
  2:12–13 are images of repentance in action. People would

rend or tear their garments as an expression of intense grief or in response to a catastrophe.[3] To *return* means to make a U-turn, to go back to the point of departure, to change one's mind.[4] What do these two words—*rend* and *return*—suggest about what it means not only to seek reconciliation with God but also to do so *with all your heart*?

• Drawing on any previous experiences of repentance and forgiveness (with God or others), what three words or phrases would you use to describe what it's like to *rend* your heart? What three words or phrases would you use to describe "the joy of being cleaned out"?

4. A crown is a symbol of honor and authority. In the Old Testament, a crown (or turban) was a mark of consecration for a priest (see Exodus 39:27–31) and a sign of sovereignty for a king (see 2 Kings 11:12). In the New Testament, the apostle Paul acknowledged the crowns given to athletes as symbols of their victory and reward (see 1 Corinthians 9:24–25). The elements of a crown, and the materials used to make it, were often significant. For instance, the number of bands around a crown might indicate the number of territories over which a king had dominion.[5] Crowns given to

kings were made of precious metals and sometimes adorned with gems (see 2 Samuel 12:30); crowns or garlands given to athletes were made of leaves or other perishable foliage (see 1 Corinthians 9:25).

- In the video, Max explored the many uses biblical writers make of thorns as symbols for the consequences of sin. Drawing on the examples of crowns in the Bible, what insights do they suggest about the significance of Jesus' crown of thorns? For example, what might a crown of thorns symbolize about the source of Jesus' authority as both priest and king? Over what did his crown give him dominion?

- The Roman soldiers who made a crown of thorns for Jesus intended it to be not only a means of physical torture but also of humiliation. However, in making it a gift of the cross, God utterly transformed it—a mock crown of pain and shame became a true crown of victory and glory. Consider the implications of receiving or declining this particular gift of the cross—of allowing God to transform whatever has been a source of pain and shame into a crown of victory and glory. What might make it difficult to truly receive this gift? What would receiving this gift require of a person throughout his or her walk with God?

5. In his allegorical novel about heaven and hell called *The Great Divorce*, author C. S. Lewis characterizes souls who set themselves against God as those who are determined to refuse the good gifts God constantly offers them.

> Good beats upon the damned incessantly as sound waves beat on the ears of the deaf, but they cannot receive it. Their fists are clenched, their teeth are clenched, their eyes fast shut. First they will not, in the end they cannot, open their hands for gifts, or their mouths for food, or their eyes to see.[6]

As you anticipate learning more about the gifts of Easter in the remaining sessions of this study, in what ways does this perspective about receiving God's gifts challenge you? In what ways does it intrigue you or encourage you?

Walking Together through Lent

6. In addition to studying together, it's also important to walk together through Lent—to share our lives with one another and to be aware of how God is at work among us. In each session, there will be many opportunities to speak life-giving—and life-challenging—words and to listen to one another deeply.

As you look ahead to the coming weeks of learning and walking together, what request would you like to make of the

group? How do you hope other members will challenge you
or encourage you? Use one or more of the sentence starters
below, or your own statement, to help the group understand
the best way to be a good friend to you throughout this study.
As each person responds, use the two-page chart that follows
to briefly note what is important to that person and how you
can be a good friend to him or her during your discussions
and times together.

> *You can help me to take Lent seriously this year by . . .*
> *I'd like you to consistently challenge me about . . .*
> *It really helps me to engage in a group when . . .*
> *I tend to withdraw or feel anxious when . . .*
> *In our discussions, the best thing you could do for*
>   *me is . . .*

Name	The Best Way I Can Be a Good Friend to This Person Is . . .

Name	The Best Way I Can Be a Good Friend to This Person Is . . .

INDIVIDUAL ACTIVITY: WHAT I WANT TO REMEMBER (2 MINUTES)

Complete this activity on your own.

1. Briefly review the outline and any notes you took.
2. In the space below, write down the most significant thing you gained in this session—from the teaching, activities, or discussions.

What I want to remember from this session . . .

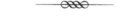

Lenten Practice

Each session in the *He Chose the Nails* study includes a Lenten practice for you to complete between sessions. Although the practice is completed on your own and outside of group time, it's a good idea to briefly preview the practice description before concluding your meeting each week. As an intentional act of preparing our hearts for Easter, the practices throughout the study require setting aside time each day to complete. To get the most out of the practice, it's important not to hurry or try to complete activities at the last minute.

CLOSING PRAYER

Close your time together with prayer.

Lenten Practice

*Let's take a good look at the way we're
living and reorder our lives under GOD.*
Lamentations 3:40 MSG

THE STARTING POINT FOR JOY

The starting point for Lent requires holding two things in tension—a humble reckoning of our sinful condition and a brave expectation that we will be changed. It is a spring-cleaning of the soul that gives us permission to take seriously the areas of our lives in which we fall short, feel defeated, or have grown cold. And it is a kindling of the soul that sparks our desire to return to God with our whole heart. The author of Hebrews captures this demanding yet joyful spirit of Lent with these words:

Let us strip off every weight that slows us down, especially the sin that so easily trips us up. And let us run with endurance the race God has set before us. We do this by keeping our eyes on Jesus, the champion who initiates and perfects our faith. Because of the joy awaiting him, he endured the cross, disregarding its shame. Now he is seated in the place of honor beside God's throne (Hebrews 12:1–2 NLT).

The Message offers a fresh perspective on this familiar passage:

Strip down, start running—and never quit! No extra spiritual fat, no parasitic sins. Keep your eyes on Jesus, who both began and finished this race we're in. Study how he did it. Because he never lost sight of where he was headed— that exhilarating finish in and with God—he could put up with anything along the way: Cross, shame, whatever. And now he's there, in the place of honor, right alongside God (Hebrews 12:1–2 MSG).

As we begin the Lenten journey in preparation for Easter, we commit to an honest examination of our lives but not to morbid introspection. We let go of hindrances but not our status as beloved children of God. In all things, we refuse to lose sight of where we're headed—an exhilarating new life with Christ. At all times, we keep our eyes fixed on Jesus and the joy before us.

The practice for this week—which you will continue and build on throughout the study—is to set aside time each day to listen to God through Scripture and prayerful reflection. The invitation is to cultivate a humble spirit of hope and expectation that God will meet you in this practice if you are willing to trust him. Author and pastor N. T. Wright writes:

> Whenever God does something new, he involves people—often unlikely people, frequently surprised and alarmed people. He asks them to trust him in a new way, to put aside their natural reactions, to listen humbly for a fresh word and to act on it without knowing exactly how it's going to work out. That's what he's asking all of us to do this Lent. Reading the Bible without knowing in advance what God is going to say takes humility . . . we may have to put our initial reactions on hold and be prepared to hear new words, to think new thoughts, and to live them out.[7]

At the beginning or end of each day this week, set aside fifteen to twenty minutes to read and prayerfully reflect on the Daily Scripture Readings (see page 29). The readings for each day are taken from the *Book of Common Prayer Daily Office* and include morning and evening psalms as well as selections from the Old Testament, New Testament epistles, and the Gospels.

- Each day, begin with a brief time of silence (one to two minutes).

- In God's loving presence, reflect for a few moments on these questions: *Where in my life am I falling short, feeling defeated, or growing cold to God? What new thing do I hope God might do in me?*

- Ask the Lord to speak to you through what you are about to read. Read the Scripture passages for the day slowly and prayerfully, paying attention to any words, phrases, or verses that stand out to you. What you're looking for is what is sometimes referred to as a "watchword"—anything that sparks a connection between the text and your life. It might be a promise, a word of wisdom, an admonition, a comfort, or an encouragement.

- Read your watchword again, receiving what you read as God's words especially for you. Then prayerfully reflect on the following questions: *What do I sense God may be saying to me? If I were to take these words seriously, how would I respond?* Spend time in silence again to listen for God, asking him to make his message clear to you.

- Use a journal or the space provided on the following pages to write down your watchword, your responses to the reflection questions, or any other observations about your experience of reading and listening for God.

- Close your time by asking God to help you "hear new words, to think new thoughts, and to live them out." Invite God to use your watchword to continue speaking to you throughout the day ahead.

- At the end of the week, review your daily reflections and observations. What stands out most to you about what God is saying to you? Write your observations in the space provided or in a journal.

Bring your notes to the next group gathering. You'll have a chance to talk about your experiences and observations at the beginning of the session 2 discussion.

DAILY SCRIPTURE READINGS

DAY 1

Morning Psalm: *Psalms 63:1–11; 98*

Old Testament: *Daniel 9:3–10*

Epistle: *Hebrews 2:10–18*

Gospel: *John 12:44–50*

Evening Psalm: *Psalm 103*

DAY 2

Morning Psalm: *Psalms 41; 52*

Old Testament: *Genesis 31:1–11*

Epistle: *1 Corinthians 1:1–19*

Gospel: *Mark 1:1–13*

Evening Psalm: *Psalm 44*

DAY 3

Morning Psalm: *Psalm 45*

Old Testament: *Genesis 37:12–24*

Epistle: *1 Corinthians 1:20–31*

Gospel: *Mark 1:14–28*

Evening Psalm: *Psalms 47–48*

DAY 4

Morning Psalm: *Psalm 119:49–72*

Old Testament: *Genesis 37:25–36*

Epistle: *1 Corinthians 2:1–13*

Gospel: *Mark 1:29–45*

Evening Psalm: *Psalms 49; 53*

DAY 5

Morning Psalm: *Psalm 50*

Old Testament: *Genesis 39:1–23*

Epistle: *1 Corinthians 2:14–3:15*

Gospel: *Mark 2:1–12*

Evening Psalm: *Psalms 59–60*

DAY 6

Morning Psalm: *Psalms 95; 40; 54*

Old Testament: *Genesis 40:1–23*

Epistle: *1 Corinthians 3:16–23*

Gospel: *Mark 2:13–22*

Evening Psalm: *Psalm 51*

DAY 7

Morning Psalm: *Psalm 55*

Old Testament: *Genesis 41:1–13*

Epistle: *1 Corinthians 4:1–7*

Gospel: *Mark 2:23–3:6*

Evening Psalm: *Psalms 138–139*

Day 1 Reflections and Observations

Day 2 Reflections and Observations

Day 3 Reflections and Observations

Day 4 Reflections and Observations

Day 5 Reflections and Observations

Day 6 Reflections and Observations

Day 7 Reflections and Observations

Week in Review

Briefly review your daily reflections and observations. What
stands out most to you about what God is saying to you?

He Chose to Forgive Us

When you were stuck in your old sin-dead
life, you were incapable of responding to
God. God brought you alive—right along
with Christ! Think of it! All sins forgiven, the
slate wiped clean, that old arrest warrant
canceled and nailed to Christ's cross.
Colossians 2:13–14 MSG

No sin is written with indelible ink.
Albert Haase, Living the Lord's Prayer

GROUP DISCUSSION: CHECKING IN (8 MINUTES)

A key part of getting to know God better is sharing your journey with others. Before watching the video, briefly check in with one another about your experiences since the last session. As time permits, discuss one or more of the following questions:

- Briefly share your experience of the session 1 practice, "The Starting Point for Joy." The focus of this practice was to set aside time each day to listen to God. How did you do? Did you find it difficult or relatively easy? Why?

- What was your experience of identifying a "watchword" each day? To what degree were you able to follow through on taking your watchwords seriously?

- Author N. T. Wright describes the necessity of putting aside our natural reactions and of reading the Bible humbly, "without knowing in advance what God is going to say." In what ways, if any, did you have to set aside your natural reactions in order to hear something new from God?

- What was it like to read and reflect on the daily Scriptures, knowing everyone else in the group was reading the same passages that day? In what ways, if any, did you find it meaningful or different than reading on your own?

VIDEO: *HE CHOSE TO FORGIVE US* (15 MINUTES)

Play the video segment for session 2. As you watch, use the outline provided to follow along or to take additional notes on anything that stands out to you.

Notes

Nails fix broken things. They join together things that were separated. They make things whole. God used nails to accomplish his plan.

The most notorious road in the world is the Via Dolorosa, the "Way of Sorrows." According to tradition, it is the route Jesus took from Pilate's hall to Calvary.

The path to the cross tells us exactly how far God will go to call us back. The nails in that cross show us the lengths God will go to cover our sins and restore our relationship with him.

Paul tells us "we were God's enemies" (Romans 5:10). An enemy is an adversary—one who offends, not out of ignorance but by intent. However, God "reconciled [us] to him through the death of his Son" (Romans 5:10) and "canceled the record that contained the charges against us. He took it and destroyed it by nailing it to Christ's cross" (Colossians 2:14 NLT).

Between Jesus' hand and the wood there was a list. A list of our mistakes: our lusts and lies and greedy moments and prodigal years.

Your sins have been blotted out by Jesus. "He has forgiven you all your sins: he has utterly wiped out the written evidence of broken commandments which always hung over our heads, and has completely annulled it by nailing it to the cross" (Colossians 2:14 PHILLIPS).

Jesus couldn't bear the thought of eternity without us—and in spite of the fact that we were his enemies—he chose the nails.

Jesus knew that the purpose of the nails was to place our sins where they could be hidden by his sacrifice and covered by his blood. As his hands opened for the nails, the doors of heaven opened for us.

GROUP DISCUSSION (35 MINUTES)

Take a few minutes to talk about what you just watched.

1. What part of the teaching had the most impact on you?

Receiving the Gift of Reconciliation

2. Imagine you have decided to give a "just because" gift to someone you know well, such as a good friend. You put a lot of thought into it and take time to create or purchase

something you are certain will make this person very happy. As the time for giving your gift approaches, you begin to imagine your recipient's reaction.

- Describe the kind of response you hope your gift recipient will have. What is the best response you could hope for— the response that would convince you that your friend has not only truly received and loved your gift but also recognized your heart in giving it?

- Now imagine a year has passed. You're helping this same friend prepare for an upcoming yard sale when you notice your gift among the items in a box designated for the sale. Which of the following would you most likely conclude?

  My friend no longer values me or our relationship as much as he/she used to.
  My friend takes me or my gift for granted.
  My friend has had a change of heart about my gift.
  My friend must not have truly received or loved my gift in the first place.
  Other:

- How might your discovery of the gift in the yard sale box impact the way you relate to your friend?

3. Max described how God left his home on a quest to bring us home. His purpose was reconciliation—to offer the gift of peace to those who were his adversaries. Here is how the apostle Paul describes the human condition and what God did for us through Christ:

> [God] made peace with everything in heaven and on earth by means of Christ's blood on the cross. This includes you who were once far away from God. You were his enemies, separated from him by your evil thoughts and actions. Yet now he has reconciled you to himself through the death of Christ in his physical body. As a result, he has brought you into his own presence, and you are holy and blameless as you stand before him without a single fault. But you must continue to believe this truth and stand firmly in it. Don't drift away from the assurance you received when you heard the Good News (Colossians 1:20–23 NLT).

Paul described our condition prior to reconciliation as that of "enemies." The Greek word Paul used was *echthros*, a derivative of the Greek word for *hatred*. Here, the literal translation of *echthros—enemies—*would be *haters*. It conveys the idea of "irreconcilable, deep-rooted enmity . . . someone from whom one can expect only harm and danger."[8]

To better understand what this enemy condition really means, set a timer for one minute and then use the space provided below to speed write a list of whoever comes to mind in connection with the phrases "enemies of God" or "God haters." For example, the list might include wicked characters from the Bible or world history, or categories of those who have committed evil acts such as human traffickers or terrorists.

After one minute, go around the group and read what you wrote, but with one addition: add the name of the person sitting on your left as the last name on your list. After everyone is done reading their lists, use the questions that follow to continue your discussion.

My list of "enemies of God" and "God haters"

- What similarities or differences do you notice about your lists? Overall, what do they suggest about your view of what it means to be an enemy of God?

- What is it like to hear your own name included on a list of God's enemies and to know that it's true—that it accurately describes your condition before you gave your life to Christ?

- In what ways, if any, are you tempted to resist, minimize, or otherwise rationalize this truth about yourself? What makes it hard to accept that it really is true?

4. Reconciliation is God's gift to his enemies.* In the passage we read in Colossians 1:20–23, the Greek word translated reconciled is *apokatallasō* whose root means to alter or exchange. In reconciliation, God offers his enemies friendship in exchange for hatred. "To reconcile," writes one theologian, "is to end a relation of enmity, and to substitute it for one of peace and goodwill."[9]

Keeping in mind the definitions of reconciliation and enemies (from question 3), read the Colossians passage again, this time from *The Message*:

All the broken and dislocated pieces of the universe—people and things, animals and atoms—get properly fixed and fit together in vibrant harmonies, all because of his death, his blood that poured down from the cross. You yourselves are a case study of what he does. At one time you all had your backs turned to God, thinking rebellious thoughts of him, giving him trouble every chance you got. But now, by giving himself completely at the Cross, actually *dying* for you, Christ brought you over to God's side and put your lives together,

---

* "All of this is a gift from God, who brought us back to himself through Christ. . . . For God was in Christ, reconciling the world to himself" (2 Corinthians 5:18–19 NLT).

whole and holy in his presence. You don't walk away
from a gift like that! You stay grounded and steady in
that bond of trust, constantly tuned in to the Message,
careful not to be distracted or diverted (Colossians
1:20–23 MSG).

- The promise of reconciliation is peace with God—we
  stand "whole and holy in his presence." This is the opposite extreme of being God's enemy. Do you find this truth
  about yourself—that you are whole and holy in God's
  sight—easier to believe and accept than the truth about
  being God's enemy? Why or why not?

- Paul acknowledges that even though we have been
  reconciled to God, it's possible to drift away from our
  assurance—to effectively walk away from God's gift. It
  makes sense that we might distance ourselves from the
  painful truth of our enemy status with God, but why
  might we also distance ourselves from the truth of our
  reconciliation?

- Briefly review the scenario in question 2, including the
  statements listed under the second bullet point. What parallels, if any, do you recognize between these statements

and the reasons we might find ourselves drifting away from the assurance of our reconciliation?

- How would you describe what it means in practical terms to "stay grounded and steady" in your reconciliation?

5. Max pointed out that it wasn't an angry mob, jealous religious leaders, or even Roman soldiers who crucified Jesus. It was Jesus himself who chose the nails. "No one can take my life from me," Jesus said, "I sacrifice it voluntarily. For I have the authority to lay it down when I want to and also to take it up again" (John 10:18 NLT).

- Why do you think it matters so much to understand this—that Jesus was not a victim but one who made a sacrificial choice from a position of authority?

- Part of the invitation of Lent is to take seriously things we might otherwise gloss over—not only the gravity of sin and our need for forgiveness but also the depth of Christ's love and the magnitude of his sacrifice for us.

Max said, "The nails in the cross show us the lengths God will go to cover our sins and restore our relationship with him." What hopes or fears come to mind when you consider taking Christ's love for you more seriously than you do right now?

Walking Together through Lent

6. At the end of the session 1 group discussion, you had the opportunity to make a request of the group and to write down the best ways you could be good friends to one another.

   • Briefly restate what you asked for from the group in session 1. What additions or clarifications would you like to make that would help the group to know more about how to be a good friend to you? As each person responds, add any additional information to the session 1 chart. (If you were absent from the last session, share your response to session 1, question 6. Then use the chart to write down what is important to each member of the group.)

   • In what ways, if any, did you find yourself responding differently to other members of the group in this session based on what they asked for in the previous session? What made that easy or difficult for you to do?

INDIVIDUAL ACTIVITY: WHAT I WANT TO REMEMBER (2 MINUTES)

Complete this activity on your own.

1. Briefly review the outline and any notes you took.

2. In the space below, write down the most significant thing you gained in this session—from the teaching, activities, or discussions.

What I want to remember from this session . . .

LENTEN PRACTICE

Before concluding, briefly review the session 2 Lenten practice, "Making Peace with God."

CLOSING PRAYER

Close your time together with prayer.

Lenten Practice

Seek GOD while he's here to be found, pray
to him while he's close at hand. . . . Come
back to GOD, who is merciful, come back to
our God, who is lavish with forgiveness.
Isaiah 55:6–7 MSG

MAKING PEACE WITH GOD

The promise of reconciliation is peace with God (see Colossians 1:19–20). And yet, as much as we want peace with God, we also might find ourselves shrinking back from it. Reconciliation requires coming to grips with sin we often prefer to minimize, overlook, or avoid. The key is to allow our sin to lead us into an even deeper immersion in the wonder of God's love and acceptance. Author and pastor Timothy Keller writes:

The gospel of justifying faith means that while Christians are, in themselves still sinful and sinning, yet in Christ, in God's sight, they are accepted and righteous. So we can say that *we are more wicked than we ever dared believe, but more loved and accepted in Christ than we ever dared hope—at the very same time.* This creates a radical new dynamic for personal growth. It means that the more you see your own flaws and sins, the more precious, electrifying, and amazing God's grace appears to you. But on the other hand, the more aware you are of God's grace and acceptance in Christ, the more able you are to drop your denials and self-defenses and admit the true dimensions and character of your sin.[10]

This week, you'll take another step in preparing your heart for Easter by seeking to make God's grace "more precious, electrifying, and amazing" through confession, and by continuing to set aside time each day to listen to God through Scripture. At the beginning or end of each day this week, set aside fifteen to twenty minutes to read and prayerfully reflect on the Daily Scripture Readings (see page 50).

- Begin with a brief time of silence (one to two minutes).

- In God's loving presence, reflect for a few moments on one or more of the following questions: *Where do I lack peace with God? For what do I need God's forgiveness? In what area of my life do I most desire to be amazed by God's grace?*
  Consider one-time failures as well as any ongoing habits of thought or behavior that come between you and God.

If you find it helpful, you may wish to refer back to your written reflections from last week in response to the question, *Where in my life am I falling short, feeling defeated, or growing cold to God?*

- With specificity, confess to God the wrong you have done or the good you have left undone. Express your regret and sorrow, asking God to forgive you and to give you "the desire and the power to do what pleases him" (Philippians 2:13 NLT). Receive God's forgiveness, expressing your wonder at the tenderness of his grace, and thanking him for his peace.

- Ask the Lord to speak to you through what you are about to read. Read the Scripture passages for the day slowly and prayerfully, paying attention to anything that sparks a connection between the text and your life. This is your "watchword" for the day. It might be a promise, a word of wisdom, an admonition, a comfort, or an encouragement.

- Read your watchword again, receiving what you read as God's words especially for you. Then, prayerfully reflect on the following questions: *What do I sense God may be saying to me? If I were to take these words seriously, how would I respond?* Spend time in silence again to listen for God, asking him to make his message clear to you.

- Use a journal or the space provided to write down your watchword, your responses to the reflection questions, or any other observations about your experience of reading and listening for God.

- Close your time by asking God to help you live in the assurance of his forgiveness and peace, and to use your watchword to continue speaking to you throughout the day ahead.

- At the end of the week, review your daily reflections and observations. What stands out most to you about what God is saying to you? Write your observations in the space provided or in a journal.

Bring your notes to the next group gathering. You'll have a chance to talk about your experiences and observations at the beginning of the session 3 discussion.

DAILY SCRIPTURE READINGS

DAY 1

Morning Psalm: *Psalms 24; 29*

Old Testament: *Genesis 41:14–45*

Epistle: *Romans 6:3–14*

Gospel: *John 5:19–24*

Evening Psalm: *Psalms 8; 84*

DAY 2

Morning Psalm: *Psalms 56–58*

Old Testament: *Genesis 41:46–57*

Epistle: *1 Corinthians 4:8–21*

Gospel: *Mark 3:7–19*

Evening Psalm: *Psalms 64–65*

DAY 3

Morning Psalm: *Psalms 61–62*

Old Testament: *Genesis 42:1–17*

Epistle: *1 Corinthians 5:1–8*

Gospel: *Mark 3:20–35*

Evening Psalm: *Psalm 68*

DAY 4

Morning Psalm: *Psalm 72*

Old Testament: *Genesis 42:18–28*

Epistle: *1 Corinthians 5:9–6:8*

Gospel: *Mark 4:1–20*

Evening Psalm: *Psalm 119:73–96*

DAY 5

Morning Psalm: *Psalms 70–71*

Old Testament: *Genesis 42:29–38*

Epistle: *1 Corinthians 6:12–20*

Gospel: *Mark 4:21–34*

Evening Psalm: *Psalm 74*

DAY 6

Morning Psalm: *Psalms 95; 69*

Old Testament: *Genesis 43:1–15*

Epistle: *1 Corinthians 7:1–9*

Gospel: *Mark 4:35–41*

Evening Psalm: *Psalm 73*

DAY 7

Morning Psalm: *Psalms 75–76*

Old Testament: *Genesis 43:16–34*

Epistle: *1 Corinthians 7:10–24*

Gospel: *Mark 5:1–20*

Evening Psalm: *Psalms 23, 27*

Day 1 Reflections and Observations

Day 2 Reflections and Observations

Day 3 Reflections and Observations

Day 4 Reflections and Observations

Day 5 Reflections and Observations

Day 6 Reflections and Observations

Day 7 Reflections and Observations

Week in Review

Briefly review your daily reflections and observations. What stands out most to you about what God is saying to you?

He Chose to Invite Us into His Presence

We are completely free to enter the Most
Holy Place without fear because of the blood
of Jesus' death. We can enter through a new
and living way that Jesus opened for us. It
leads through the curtain—Christ's body.
Hebrews 10:19–20 NCV

The cross of Jesus tears apart that veil and lets
us see inside the Holy of Holies, the heart of
God. And what do we see there? Unfathomable
love, unfathomable forgiveness, a compassion
and tenderness beyond understanding.
Ronald Rolheiser, "The Cross as
Revealing God's Unconditional Love"

GROUP DISCUSSION: CHECKING IN (8 MINUTES)

A key part of getting to know God better is sharing your journey with others. Before watching the video, briefly check in with one another about your experiences since the last session. As time permits, discuss one or more of the following questions:

- Briefly share your experience of the session 2 practice, "Making Peace with God." The focus of this practice was confession. What was it like to reflect on your life, to practice confession, and to receive God's forgiveness?

- In what ways, if any, did practicing confession and receiving forgiveness help you to experience God's grace as "more precious, electrifying, and amazing"?

- What was the most meaningful or helpful watchword you identified in your daily Scripture reading? How did God use it to challenge, encourage, or comfort you?

- What similarities or differences do you notice among the watchwords each of you identified this week?

VIDEO: *HE CHOSE TO INVITE US INTO HIS PRESENCE* (15 MINUTES)

Play the video segment for session 3. As you watch, use the outline provided to follow along or to take additional notes on anything that stands out to you.

Notes

Morally, how we "dress" ourselves—the ethics and convictions we embrace—shapes our attitude, choices, and behavior. It indicates to others who we really are . . . on the inside.

As we prepare to live out the part God wants us to play, it might be a good idea to look in the mirror and ask the question, "What clothes am I wearing?"

Jesus not only offered us his own robe but also invited us into his Father's presence. . . . What once separated us from his presence has been removed. Nothing remains between us and God but an open door (see Hebrews 10:19–20 NCV).

Jesus hasn't left us with an unapproachable God. Yes, God is holy. Yes, we are sinful. But Jesus is our mediator. He was the curtain between us and God, and his flesh was torn for you and me. "When Jesus had cried out again in a loud voice, he gave up his spirit. At that moment the curtain of the temple was torn in two from top to bottom" (Matthew 27:50–51).

Though there is no curtain in a temple, there is a curtain in the heart. Our guilty conscience becomes a curtain that separates us from God. As a result, we hide from our Master.

Somewhere, sometime, somehow, you got tangled up in garbage, and you've been avoiding God. You've allowed a veil of guilt to come between you and your Father.

You came to the cross dressed in sin, but you leave dressed in the "coat of his strong love" (Isaiah 59:17 NCV), girded with a belt of "goodness and fairness" (Isaiah 11:5 NCV), and clothed in "garments of salvation" (Isaiah 61:10). Indeed, you leave dressed in Christ himself!

GROUP DISCUSSION (35 MINUTES)

Take a few minutes to talk about what you just watched.

1. What part of the teaching had the most impact on you?

Receiving the Gift of God's Presence

2. Imagine you have been offered the opportunity to spend an hour with someone you admire and respect but have never met. It might be a favorite musician, author, leader, scholar, artist, athlete, entrepreneur, or an expert in a given field.

   • Briefly describe who your admired person is and how you would most enjoy spending your time with him or her. What would you like to do together? What would you most like to talk about?

   • Now imagine that when you arrive for your appointment, you are told that although you will indeed be spending an hour with your admired person, there will be a curtain between the two of you the entire time. How would it change the way you had hoped to spend your time together? To what degree would the curtain diminish your ability to enjoy the visit? A little, a lot, or somewhere between?

3. Max used the image of Jesus' robe to describe what Jesus did for us on the cross: in exchange for our garments of sin he gave us his robe of seamless perfection, a symbol of the righteousness that gives us access to God's presence. For the Jews of Jesus' day, God's presence resided solely in the temple—specifically, the innermost room of the temple called the Holy of Holies or the Most Holy Place. Because God was holy and his people were not, thick curtains provided a separation barrier between them.* Here is how the writer of Hebrews describes this innermost part of the temple:

> In its first room were the lampstand and the table with its consecrated bread; this was called the Holy Place. Behind the second curtain was a room called the Most Holy Place. . . . The priests entered regularly into the outer room to carry on their ministry. But only the high priest entered the inner room, and that only once a year, and never without blood, which he offered for himself

---

* "A symbol of God's unapproachability, this curtain was made of blue, purple, scarlet, and fine twisted linen embroidered with figures of cherubim (Exodus 26:31–37; 36:35). It was hung with golden hooks upon four pillars of acacia wood overlaid with gold which were set in sockets or bases of silver. It is likely that the curtain was quite thick to correspond with its great size." "Curtain," in *Zondervan Illustrated Bible Dictionary*, ed. J. D. Douglas and Merrill C. Tenney, revised by Moisés Silva (Grand Rapids: Zondervan, 1987, 2011), 323.

and for the sins the people had committed in ignorance (Hebrews 9:2-3, 6-7).

One of the most vivid images we have of Jesus breaking down the sin barrier that separated us from God happened in this innermost part of the temple at the very moment of his death: "And when Jesus had cried out again in a loud voice, he gave up his spirit. At that moment the curtain of the temple was torn in two from top to bottom" (Matthew 27:50–51). With the temple curtain torn, there was no longer a separation barrier between the people and God's presence in the Most Holy Place. The writer of Hebrews uses the image of the torn curtain to explain how Christ's death on the cross gives us access to God's presence:

> Christ did not go into the Most Holy Place made by humans, which is only a copy of the real one. He went into heaven itself and is there now before God to help us. The high priest enters the Most Holy Place once every year with blood that is not his own. But Christ did not offer himself many times. Then he would have had to suffer many times since the world was made. But Christ came only once and for all time at just the right time to take away all sin by sacrificing himself. . . . We are completely free to enter the Most Holy Place without fear because of the blood of Jesus' death. We can enter through a new and living way that Jesus opened for us. It leads through the curtain—Christ's body (Hebrews 9:24–26; 10:19–20 NCV).

- For the Jews of Jesus' day, it would have been unthinkable that God's presence could reside outside the temple or that anyone other than a priest would have access to it. In what ways do you recognize remnants of this mind-set among people today? For example, what kinds of things—places, people, events, or activities—are thought to be holier and closer to God than others?

- Overall, would you say that this mindset tends to be more prevalent or less prevalent among Christians? Share the reasons for your response.

- How does the parallel between the temple curtain and Christ's body help you understand what Christ's death on the cross really accomplished? What might have been less clear or harder to understand if the temple curtain had not been torn?

- What, if anything, appeals to you or intrigues you about the ancient Most Holy Place—of having a fixed physical location for God's presence?

- What comes to mind when you imagine yourself stepping into the Most Holy Place in the temple? In what ways, if any, does imagining yourself there physically shift your perspective on what it means to access God's presence in your everyday life?

4. Because direct access to God's presence is a foundational and familiar teaching of the Christian faith, there are times when we might take it for granted, or struggle to grasp its significance. Author and pastor Eugene Peterson elaborates on what direct access to God's presence really means for us:

> The "Holy of Holies" [was] the place where the focused action between God and humans took place. . . . No one was permitted into the Holy of Holies except the High Priest, and then only once a year. The holy and the profane were strictly separated. . . . And so the shock is nothing less than seismic to be told that the first thing that happened when Jesus died on the cross was that "the curtain of the temple was torn in two, from top to bottom."
>
> What happened? The Holy Place is now Every Place. The Holy One of God is contemporary With Us. His time is our time. There is no more separation between there and here, then and now, sacred and secular . . . the death of Jesus on the cross open[s] up "a new and living way" by which we can live an integrated life.[11]

- Because Christ's sacrifice gives us access to God's presence, we can live what Peterson describes as "an integrated life." To *integrate* something is to create a unified whole from once separate things. It means in part that every place can be a holy place—no place is off limits and no moment is too small for God's presence. What comes to mind when you consider what this truth might mean for you *right now*—in this very place, at this very moment?

- The good news is that we can live an integrated life. The challenge is that we sometimes default to a dis-integrated or compartmentalized life with God instead. Perhaps without even realizing it, we live as if . . .

  God is in holy places but not in every place.
  God was at work in that time but not in our time.
  God is present over there but not right here.
  God could show up then but not now.
  God is present in sacred things but not in secular things.

  Which of these statements represents a compartmentalization you are most likely to default to?

How would you describe the purpose of the "curtain" or separation barrier this compartmentalization represents? What integration or wholeness might you be shielding yourself from?

5. Max pointed out that guilt is a curtain of the heart we sometimes use to shield ourselves from God's presence. Just as Max's guilty dog avoided him after foraging through the trash, a guilty conscience can separate us from God.

- Which of the following statements comes closest to describing what you tend to shield yourself from when guilt comes between you and God? Share the reasons for your response.

When I put up guilt as a curtain . . .

> *I am shielding myself from my expectation of God's anger or disapproval.*
> *I am shielding myself from facing God until I can get my act together.*
> *I am shielding myself from my own shame.*
> *I am shielding myself from confessing my failure.*
> *I am shielding myself from making restitution to others.*
> *I am shielding myself from making necessary changes.*
> Other:

- "God isn't angry with you," Max said. "He's already dealt with your mistake. The door is open and God invites you in." As you consider the statement you identified with above, how would you describe God's invitation to you when you use guilt as a shield? At those times, what might choosing an integrated life—dropping the curtain—require of you?

Walking Together through Lent

6. Take a few moments to reflect on what you've learned and experienced together in this study so far.

   - How has learning more about the gifts of the cross impacted you or your relationship with God?

   - Since the first session, what shifts have you noticed in yourself in terms of how you relate to the group? For example, do you feel more or less guarded, understood, challenged, encouraged, connected?

- What adjustments, if any, would you like to make to the session 1 chart that would help other members of the group know how to be a good friend to you?

INDIVIDUAL ACTIVITY: WHAT I WANT TO REMEMBER (2 MINUTES)

Complete this activity on your own.

1. Briefly review the outline and any notes you took.
2. In the space below, write down the most significant thing you gained in this session—from the teaching, activities, or discussions.

What I want to remember from this session . . .

LENTEN PRACTICE

Before concluding, briefly review the session 3 Lenten practice, "Clothed with Christ in God's Presence."

CLOSING PRAYER

Close your time together with prayer.

Lenten Practice

By faith in Christ you are in direct relationship with God. Your baptism in Christ
was not just washing you up for a fresh
start. It also involved dressing you in an
adult faith wardrobe—Christ's life, the
fulfillment of God's original promise.
Galatians 3:26–27 MSG

CLOTHED WITH CHRIST
IN GOD'S PRESENCE

In the group session, Max described how Christ not only offered
us his own robe of perfection but also invited us into God's presence. Jesus wore our sin so we could wear his righteousness, and
we leave the cross dressed in the "coat of his strong love" (Isaiah

59:17 NCV). Through his death, Christ destroyed the barrier that once separated us from God, and we now have direct access to God's presence. The challenge and opportunity we have each day is to live in conscious awareness of God's presence with us. Author and pastor A.W. Tozer writes:

> God wills that we should push on into his Presence and live our whole life there. This is to be known to us in conscious experience. It is more than a doctrine to be held, it is a life to be enjoyed every moment of every day. . . . The greatest fact of the tabernacle was that Jehovah was there; a Presence was waiting within the veil. Similarly the Presence of God is the central fact of Christianity. At the heart of the Christian message is God himself waiting for his redeemed children to push in to conscious awareness of his Presence.[12]

In addition to continuing the practice of reflection on Scripture, this week you'll use your daily routine of getting dressed as a prompt to "put on the Lord Jesus Christ" (Romans 13:14 NASB) and to increase your awareness of God's presence with you.

As you dress each day, allow each piece of clothing to serve as a reminder that you are dressed in the "coat of his strong love" and therefore have ceaseless access to God's presence. If you find it helpful, write the following prayer by A. W. Tozer on a card or Post-it note and place it on a mirror or in a closet or dresser drawer: "Lord, increase my curiosity and help me to know you so intimately that I am especially, specifically, consciously aware of your presence throughout the day."[13] For a midday prompt, use the prayer to create an alert on your smartphone, tablet, or laptop.

At the beginning or end of each day this week, set aside fifteen to twenty minutes to read and prayerfully reflect on the Daily Scripture Readings (see page 73).

- Begin with a brief time of silence (one to two minutes).

- In God's loving presence, reflect for a few moments on one or more of the following questions: *In the last twenty-four hours, when was I consciously aware of God's presence? When do I wish I had been consciously aware of God's presence?*

- Ask the Lord to speak to you through what you are about to read. Read the Scripture passages for the day slowly and prayerfully, paying attention to anything that sparks a connection between the text and your life. This is your "watchword" for the day. It might be a promise, a word of wisdom, an admonition, a comfort, or an encouragement.

- Read your watchword again, receiving what you read as God's words especially for you. Then prayerfully reflect on these questions: *What do I sense God may be saying to me? If I were to take these words seriously, how would I respond?* Spend time in silence again to listen for God, asking him to make his message clear to you.

- Use a journal or the space provided to write down your watchword, your responses to the reflection questions, or any other observations about your experience of reading and listening for God.

- Close your time by asking God to help you "put on Christ" this day and to be consciously aware of his presence with you. Invite him to use your watchword to continue speaking to you throughout the day ahead.

- At the end of the week, review your daily reflections and observations. What stands out most to you about what God is saying to you? Write your observations in the space provided or in a journal.

Bring your notes to the next group gathering. You'll have a chance to talk about your experiences and observations at the beginning of the session 4 discussion.

DAILY SCRIPTURE READINGS

DAY 1

Morning Psalm: *Psalms 93; 96*

Old Testament: *Genesis 44:1–17*

Epistle: *Romans 8:1–10*

Gospel: *John 5:25–29*

Evening Psalm: *Psalm 34*

DAY 2

Morning Psalm: *Psalm 80*

Old Testament: *Genesis 44:18–34*

Epistle: *1 Corinthians 7:25–31*

Gospel: *Mark 5:21–43*

Evening Psalm: *Psalms 77; 79*

DAY 3

Morning Psalm: *Psalm 78:1–39*

Old Testament: *Genesis 45:1–15*

Epistle: *1 Corinthians 7:32–40*

Gospel: *Mark 6:1–13*

Evening Psalm: *Psalm 78:40–72*

DAY 4

Morning Psalm: *Psalm 119:97–120*

Old Testament: *Genesis 45:16–28*

Epistle: *1 Corinthians 8:1–13*

Gospel: *Mark 6:14–29*

Evening Psalm: *Psalms 81–82*

DAY 5

Morning Psalm: *Psalm 42*

Old Testament: *Genesis 46:1–7, 28–34*

Epistle: *1 Corinthians 9:1–15*

Gospel: *Mark 6:30–46*

Evening Psalm: *Psalms 85–86*

DAY 6

Morning Psalm: *Psalms 95; 88*

Old Testament: *Genesis 47:1–26*

Epistle: *1 Corinthians 9:16–27*

Gospel: *Mark 6:47–56*

Evening Psalm: *Psalms 91–92*

DAY 7

Morning Psalm: *Psalms 87; 90*

Old Testament: *Genesis 47:27–48:7*

Epistle: *1 Corinthians 10:1–13*

Gospel: *Mark 7:1–23*

Evening Psalm: *Psalm 136*

Day 1 Reflections and Observations

Day 2 Reflections and Observations

Day 3 Reflections and Observations

Day 4 Reflections and Observations

Day 5 Reflections and Observations

Day 6 Reflections and Observations

Day 7 Reflections and Observations

Week in Review

Briefly review your daily reflections and observations. What stands out most to you about what God is saying to you?

SESSION 4

He Chose to Love Us Forever

This is how we know what love is:
Jesus Christ laid down his life for us.
1 John 3:16

To follow Jesus implies that we enter into a
way of life that is given character and shape
and direction by the one who calls us.
Eugene H. Peterson, The Jesus Way

GROUP DISCUSSION: CHECKING IN (8 MINUTES)

A key part of getting to know God better is sharing your journey with others. Before watching the video, briefly check in with one another about your experiences since the last session. As time permits, discuss one or more of the following questions:

- Briefly share your experience of the session 3 practice, "Clothed with Christ in God's Presence." The focus of this practice was to use your daily routine of getting dressed as a prompt to be aware of God's presence. To what degree did the practice help to increase your awareness of God's presence not only at the start of the day but throughout it?

- Did increasing your awareness of God's presence impact the way you experienced your day (i.e., your state of mind, the choices you made, the way you related to others)?

- What was the most meaningful or helpful watchword you identified in your daily Scripture reading? How did God use it to challenge, encourage, or comfort you?

- What similarities or differences do you notice among the watchwords each of you identified this week?

VIDEO: *HE CHOSE TO LOVE US FOREVER* (16 MINUTES)

Play the video segment for session 4. As you watch, use the outline provided to follow along or to take additional notes on anything that stands out to you.

Notes

The cross was a gift from God.

He has provided two kinds of sanctification to us:

Positional sanctification: Christ's work *for* us. We are given a prize not because of what we do but because of who we know.

Progressive sanctification: Christ's work *in* us. We are continuously transformed by God.

The cross is the universal symbol of Christianity. The design couldn't be simpler: one beam represents the width of God's love, and the other reflects the height of his holiness.

The cross is where God forgave his children without lowering his standards.

The sin is punished, but we are safe in the shadow of the cross. We were "made holy through the sacrifice Christ made in his body once and for all time" (Hebrews 10:10).

We are *positionally sanctified*—the achievement of Jesus' blood is credited to us. We are also *progressively sanctified*—his work in us is ongoing. We can't be more saved than we were the day we accepted Christ's sacrifice on the cross and received salvation—but we can grow in that salvation.

As boldly as the center beam proclaims God's holiness, the crossbeam declares his love.

Because of God's love for all of us, we can engrave in our hearts the truth that Jesus is "the Lamb of God, who takes away the sin of the world" (John 1:29).

Because of God's love, the blood of Christ does not just cover our sins, or conceal our sins, or postpone our sins, or diminish our sins. It takes away our sins, once and for all time. . . . Jesus allows our mistakes to be lost in his perfection.

GROUP DISCUSSION (34 MINUTES)

Take a few minutes to talk about what you just watched.

1. What part of the teaching had the most impact on you?

Receiving the Gift of Sanctification

2. Max used the structure of the cross to describe how God forgave us without lowering his standards: "One beam reaches out, representing the width of God's love," he said, "and

the other reflects the heights of his holiness. The cross is the intersection of his love and his holiness." The apostle Paul provides a beautiful description of God's work on the cross when he writes, "You were washed, you were sanctified, you were justified in the name of the Lord Jesus Christ and by the Spirit of our God" (1 Corinthians 6:11). Paul stresses the miracle of what God did for us on the cross with three distinct Greek words:

> (1) *apolousasthe* (washed): to be washed entirely (not just a part), especially the removal of dirt; spiritually cleansed and purified by God.
>
> (2) *hēgiasthēte* (sanctified): made holy, consecrated, set apart for a purpose.
>
> (3) *edikaiōthēte* (justified): declared righteous, not guilty (in a legal sense); approved by God and conforming to God's standard.[14]

- We all come to God in unique ways—some as children, others as adults; some through the intensity of a crisis, others through the quiet routines of life; some at a specific point in time, others during a broader season of life. Overall, how would you describe the journey that brought you to the cross?

- As you reflect on your own experience of surrendering your life to Christ, which of Paul's three words in

1 Corinthians 6:11 do you relate to most or find most meaningful?

- How would you characterize the role your conversion experience plays in your life with God in this season of your life? For example, if you've been a Christian for many years, it may be that you don't often think of it or perhaps take it for granted. If you're a new believer, it may be a daily source of joy, gratitude, and strength.

3. Max described two kinds of sanctification: *positional sanctification*, which is God's work *for* us; and *progressive sanctification*, which is God's work *in* us. Here is how theologian Wayne Grudem briefly summarizes the two.[15]

Positional Sanctification (Justification)	Progressive Sanctification (Transformation)
A legal standing	An internal condition
Once for all time	Continuous throughout life
Entirely God's work	We cooperate
Perfect in this life	Not perfect in this life
The same in all Christians	Greater in some than in others

- Of the five contrasts on the chart, which do you find most helpful or clarifying? Share the reasons for your response.

- In what ways, if any, would you say we sometimes confuse the two?

- How would you describe the potential outcome of neglecting either one?

4. "We can't be more saved than we were the day we accepted Christ's sacrifice on the cross and received salvation," Max said, "but we can grow in that salvation." In his second letter to the church at Corinth, the apostle Paul beautifully acknowledges the reality of such progressive sanctification, the expectation that we are continuously transformed by Christ: "And the Lord—who is the Spirit—makes us more and more like him as we are changed into his glorious image" (2 Corinthians 3:18 NLT).

   The Message puts it this way:

And so we are transfigured much like the Messiah, our lives gradually becoming brighter and more beautiful as God enters our lives and we become like him (2 Corinthians 3:18 MSG).

The root of the Greek word Paul uses for *changed* is *metamorphoō*, which is also the source of the English word *metamorphosis*. A metamorphosis is a complete and profound change that happens through growth. In the natural world, metamorphosis is what occurs when a tadpole becomes a frog or a caterpillar becomes a butterfly.

• The kind of life-change metamorphosis implies is radical—from one form into another—but it is also gradual. What makes this kind of radical-gradual spiritual growth uniquely challenging?

• What desires or hopes does the promise of metamorphosis stir in you? For example, in what ways do you long for your life to be brighter, more beautiful?

• The process of change can be discouraging because we can't always see it when we're in the midst of it. As you reflect on your life with God, what is one gradual but significant change you've experienced over time, and what insights might this experience provide as an encouragement for any gradual changes you're working through now?

5. Progressive sanctification includes not only the expectation of growth but also of an increasing aversion to and freedom from sin. "We obey God and shrink back from all that displeases him," Max said. In his letter to the church at Ephesus, the apostle Paul uses the image of light to help his readers understand what living out their salvation in this way requires of them: "For once you were darkness, but now in the Lord you are light. Live as children of light—for the fruit of the light is found in all that is good and right and true. Try to find out what is pleasing to the Lord" (Ephesians 5:8–10 NRSV).

To better understand what it looks like in practical terms to live this way, consider how author and pastor Dallas Willard describes some of the characteristics of children of light:

> Whenever they are found to be in the wrong, they will never defend it—neither to themselves nor to others, much less to God. They are thankful to be found out.
>
> They do not feel they are missing out on something good by not sinning. They are not disappointed and do not feel deprived.

[They are] mainly governed by the pull of the good. Their energy is not invested in *not* doing what is wrong, but in doing what is good.

Life in the path of rightness becomes easy and joyous.[16]

- Paul could have used the phrase "*people* of light" instead of "*children* of light." What nuances might his use of *children* suggest about what living in light requires of us?

- Take a moment to think of anyone you know in whom you have observed one or more of the four characteristics Willard describes. What specifically did you observe about that person? How did his or her life demonstrate the fruit of light—all that is good and right and true?

- Recall a recent time when you were found to be in the wrong. In what ways, if any, did you defend yourself—to yourself, to others, or to God? Or, how did you respond with gratitude at being found out?

- Which of the four characteristics Willard describes do you feel most intrigued by or drawn to? Share the reasons for your response.

Walking Together through Lent

6. Christ demonstrated his love for us on the cross, but his love didn't stop there. Every day, he invites us to receive his love anew and to be changed by it. As you continue to journey through Lent to Easter, in what ways or in what areas of life are you most aware of your need to receive God's love? How do you hope (or fear) you might be changed by that love?

INDIVIDUAL ACTIVITY: WHAT I WANT TO REMEMBER (2 MINUTES)

Complete this activity on your own.

1. Briefly review the outline and any notes you took.
2. In the space below, write down the most significant thing you gained in this session—from the teaching, activities, or discussions.

What I want to remember from this session . . .

LENTEN PRACTICE

Before concluding, briefly review the session 4 Lenten Practice, "The Pull of the Good."

CLOSING PRAYER

Close your time together with prayer.

Get a Head Start on the
Session 5 Discussion

As part of the group discussion for session 5, you'll have an opportunity to talk about what you've learned and experienced together throughout the *He Chose the Nails* study. Between now and your next meeting, take a few moments to review the previous sessions and identify the teaching, discussions, or practices that stand out most to you. Use the worksheet on the following pages to briefly summarize the highlights of what you've learned and experienced.

HEAD START WORKSHEET

Take a few moments to reflect on what you've learned and experienced throughout the *He Chose the Nails* study. You may want to review notes from the video teaching, what you wrote down for "What I Want to Remember" at the end of each group session, and observations from weekly practice notes. Here are some questions you might consider as part of your review:

- What insights did I gain from this session?
- What was the most important thing I learned about myself in this session?
- How did this session help me to prepare my heart for Easter?
- How did I experience God's presence or leading related to this session?
- How did this session impact my relationships with the other people in the group?

Use the spaces provided below and on the next page to briefly summarize what you've learned and experienced for each session.

Session 1: He Chose to Be One of Us

Session 2: He Chose to Forgive Us

Session 3: He Chose to Invite Us into His Presence

Session 4: He Chose to Love Us Forever

Lenten Practice

And so we are transfigured much like the
Messiah, our lives gradually becoming
brighter and more beautiful as God enters
our lives and we become like him.

2 Corinthians 3:18 MSG

THE PULL OF THE GOOD

In the group session, Max described two kinds of sanctification: positional sanctification (God's work *for* us) and progressive sanctification (God's work *in* us). Progressive sanctification includes all the ways we grow to become more like Christ. It also includes the expectation of an increasing aversion to and freedom from sin. The challenge is that in our efforts to avoid sin, it's possible to give sin *more* space in our lives rather than less. Author and pastor John Ortberg writes:

> Many Christians expend so much energy and worry trying
> not to sin. The goal is not to try to sin less. In all your efforts
> to keep from sinning, what are you focusing on? Sin. God
> wants you to focus on him.[17]

The alternative to expending too much energy on trying not to sin is to switch our focus from sin to God, and to the good, which is how Dallas Willard describes one of the key characteristics of children of light: "[They are] mainly governed by the pull of the good. Their energy is not invested in *not* doing what is wrong, but in doing what is good."[18]

This week, in addition to your daily reflections on Scripture, you'll continue to prepare your heart for Easter by shifting your focus from trying hard *not* to sin, to being "governed by the pull of the good."

Identify an area of life in which you feel vulnerable to doing what is wrong or behaving in a regrettable way. The context might be a personal struggle, a difficult relationship, or a challenging circumstance. Allow this situation to be your focus for seeking to be governed by the good this week. If you find it helpful, write a reminder on a Post-it note or create an alert on an electronic device. For example, "Live as a child of light," "Focus on the pull of the good," or "Lord, give me the desire and the power to do what pleases you."

At the beginning or end of each day this week, set aside fifteen to twenty minutes to read and prayerfully reflect on the Daily Scripture Readings (see page 97).

- Begin with a brief time of silence (one to two minutes).

- In God's loving presence, reflect for a few moments on one or more of the following questions: *In what ways was I governed by the pull of the good yesterday? In what ways did I fail to be governed by the pull of the good yesterday? Where am I most vulnerable to doing what is wrong or regrettable today? How might I invest my energy in doing what is good instead?*

- Ask the Lord to speak to you through what you are about to read. Read the Scripture passages for the day slowly and prayerfully, paying attention to anything that sparks a connection between the text and your life. This is your "watchword" for the day. It might be a promise, a word of wisdom, an admonition, a comfort, or an encouragement.

- Read your watchword again, receiving what you read as God's words especially for you. Then, prayerfully reflect on the following questions: *What do I sense God may be saying to me? If I were to take these words seriously, how would I respond?* Spend time in silence again to listen for God, asking him to make his message clear to you.

- Use a journal or the space provided to write down your watchword, your responses to the reflection questions, or any other observations about your experience of reading and listening for God.

- Close your time by asking God to give you "the desire and the power to do what pleases him" (Philippians 2:13 NLT), and to use your watchword to continue speaking to you throughout the day ahead.

- At the end of the week, review your daily reflections and observations. What stands out most to you about what God is saying to you? Write your observations in the space provided or in a journal.

Bring your notes to the next group gathering. You'll have a chance to talk about your experiences and observations at the beginning of the session 5 discussion.

DAILY SCRIPTURE READINGS

DAY 1

Morning Psalm: *Psalms 66–67*
Old Testament: *Genesis 48:8–22*
Epistle: *Romans 8:11–25*
Gospel: *John 6:27–40*
Evening Psalm: *Psalms 19; 46*

DAY 2

Morning Psalm: *Psalm 89:1–18*
Old Testament: *Genesis 49:1–28*
Epistle: *1 Corinthians 10:14–11:1*
Gospel: *Mark 7:24–37*
Evening Psalm: *Psalm 89:19–52*

DAY 3

Morning Psalm: *Psalms 97; 99*
Old Testament: *Genesis 49:29–50:14*
Epistle: *1 Corinthians 11:17–34*
Gospel: *Mark 8:1–10*
Evening Psalm: *Psalm 94*

DAY 4

Morning Psalm: *Psalms 101; 109*
Old Testament: *Genesis 50:15–26*
Epistle: *1 Corinthians 12:1–11*
Gospel: *Mark 8:11–26*
Evening Psalm: *Psalm 119:121–144*

DAY 5

Morning Psalm: *Psalm 69*
Old Testament: *Exodus 1:6–22*
Epistle: *1 Corinthians 12:12–26*
Gospel: *Mark 8:27–9:1*
Evening Psalm: *Psalm 73*

DAY 6

Morning Psalm: *Psalms 95; 102*
Old Testament: *Exodus 2:1–22*
Epistle: *1 Corinthians 12:27–13:3*
Gospel: *Mark 9:2–13*
Evening Psalm: *Psalms 91–92*

DAY 7

Morning Psalm: *Psalms 107:33–108:13*
Old Testament: *Exodus 2:23–3:15*
Epistle: *1 Corinthians 13:1–13*
Gospel: *Mark 9:14–29*
Evening Psalm: *Psalm 33*

Day 1 Reflections and Observations

Day 2 Reflections and Observations

Day 3 Reflections and Observations

Day 4 Reflections and Observations

Day 5 Reflections and Observations

Day 6 Reflections and Observations

Day 7 Reflections and Observations

Week in Review

Briefly review your daily reflections and observations. What stands out most to you about what God is saying to you?

SESSION 5

He Chose to Give Us Victory

Overwhelming victory is ours
through Christ, who loved us.
Romans 8:37 NLT

Jesus came in the flesh and he suffered all
of the things that people suffer in the flesh.
He does this so that we can go with him
to the cross, and we can participate in the
brokenness of this life so we can see and
enter into the resurrection of Jesus and be a
part of that. . . . It is through death that we
enter into the victory that is beyond death.
Dallas Willard, "A Conversation
on Pain and Suffering"

GROUP DISCUSSION:
CHECKING IN (8 MINUTES)

A key part of getting to know God better is sharing your journey with others. Before watching the video, briefly check in with one another about your experiences since the last session. As time permits, use one or more of the following questions:

- Briefly share your experience of the session 4 practice, "The Pull of the Good." The focus of this practice was to shift your focus from trying hard *not* to sin to being "governed by the pull of the good" instead. What did you find most challenging about shifting your focus in this way? What did you learn about yourself in the process?

- What was the most meaningful or helpful watchword you identified in your daily Scripture reading? How did God use it to challenge, encourage, or comfort you?

- What similarities or differences do you notice among the watchwords each of you identified this week?

VIDEO: *HE CHOSE TO GIVE US VICTORY* (18 MINUTES)

Play the video segment for session 5. As you watch, use the outline provided to follow along or to take additional notes on anything that stands out to you.

Notes

The decisions we all face in our lives are like the notes on the page. Our instrument can be used to bemoan tragedy or sing praise and triumph. How we play our song is our choice. But a decision must be made.

Just before Jesus died, he asked for something to drink. But he refused myrrh and gall. He refused to be stupefied by the drugs, opting instead to feel the full force of his suffering. Why? Because he knew we'd face pain—if not the pain of the body, the pain of the soul. He knew we'd face thirst. If not a thirst for water, at least a thirst for truth.

Because John lingered on Saturday, he was around on Sunday to see the miracle. What did he see? "Strips of linen" (John 20:5). Through the rags of death, John saw the power of life. John would tell you God can turn any tragedy into a triumph, if only you wait and watch.

In order for the cross of Christ to be the cross of our lives, we need to bring something to the hill. We can bring our *bad moments* and our *mad moments*: bad habits, selfish moods, white lies, binges, and bigotries.

The first step after a stumble must be in the direction of the cross. "If we confess our sins to God, he can always be trusted to forgive us and take our sins away" (1 John 1:9 CEV).

God wants our worries as well. We can bring the fears we have about our *final moments*. He wants us to trust him. "Don't let your hearts be troubled," he urges us. "I will come back and take you to be with me so that you may be where I am" (John 14:1, 3).

If God can change the disciples' lives through a tragedy such as the cross and the tomb, could it be he will use a tragedy to change yours? As hard as it may be to believe, you could be only a Saturday away from a resurrection.

GROUP DISCUSSION (32 MINUTES)

Take a few minutes to talk about what you just watched.

1. What part of the teaching had the most impact on you?

Receiving the Gift of Victory

2. The victory accomplished through Christ's death and resurrection is sometimes referred to as the "paschal mystery." The word *paschal* (*pas-kuhl*) comes from the Greek word for *Passover*, the Jewish remembrance of when the angel of death "passed over" the Hebrew families prior to their exodus from slavery in Egypt (see Exodus 12:13, 23).

   The lamb sacrificed and eaten at Jewish Passover celebrations was the paschal lamb, a term New Testament writers also use for Christ (see John 1:29; 1 Corinthians 5:7). The paschal mystery encompasses God's hidden plan of salvation revealed in Christ's death, burial, and resurrection.[19] In his first letter to the church at Corinth, the apostle Paul summarizes the events of the paschal mystery when he writes:

> Christ died for our sins, just as the Scriptures said. He was buried, and he was raised from the dead on the third day, just as the Scriptures said (1 Corinthians 15:3–4 NLT).

The paschal mystery is also understood as the recurring pattern of God's transforming work in our lives: that some form of death always precedes new life—and that death never has the last word. Speaking of the life that would follow his own death, Jesus said to his disciples: "I tell you the truth, unless a kernel of wheat is planted in the soil and dies, it remains alone. But its death will produce many new kernels—a plentiful harvest of new lives" (John 12:24 NLT).

- For a seed, there is life on both sides of death (planting), but each life is of a very different kind. What three words or phrases would you use to describe the life of the seed before death? What three words or phrases would you use to describe the life that follows death?

- What parallels do you recognize between life on either side of death for the seed and the before-and-after life human beings experience whenever we encounter some form of death (a tragedy, a personal struggle, a choice to deny ourselves, etc.)? In what ways might the same two sets of words and phrases you used for seeds also apply to the human experience on either side of a death?

- Overall, what does God's paschal pattern—in the natural world and in the life of Christ—suggest about what "victory" is when we experience some form of death in our lives?

3. Author and pastor Eugene Peterson comments on God's paschal work in our lives when he writes, "All suffering, all pain, all emptiness, all disappointment is seed: sow it in God and he will, finally, bring a crop of joy from it."[20]

- If we think of the hardships and losses of this life as seeds, we have at least three options for what we can do with them: (1) we can cling to our seeds and refuse to sow them; (2) we can sow our seeds in God; or (3) we can sow our seeds in something other than God. In practical terms, how would you describe what it means to follow through on each option?

- Of the three options, which comes closest to describing your tendency when you are in a season of hardship? Are you more likely to cling to life as it is, surrender yourself to God in faith, or try to bury yourself in distractions or self-defeating behaviors?

4. Speaking of Jesus' empty grave clothes, Max said, "God took a token of tragedy and turned it into a symbol of triumph." We all face tragedy and hardships, but the promise of Scripture is that God is always at work to bring victory and new life, even from the rags of death. The apostle Paul writes:

> And we know that God causes everything to work together for the good of those who love God and are called according to his purpose for them. . . . Can anything ever separate us from Christ's love? Does it mean he no longer loves us if we have trouble or calamity, or are persecuted, or hungry, or destitute, or in danger, or threatened with death? . . . No, despite all these things, overwhelming victory is ours through Christ, who loved us (Romans 8:28, 35, 37 NLT).

The phrase translated "overwhelming victory" is a compound of two Greek words, *hyper* and *nikaō*. *Nikaō* means "to be victorious," and *hyper* is an intensifier of whatever it precedes: "Overwhelming victory [*hypernikaō*] is ours through Christ, who loved us" (Romans 8:37 NLT).

You may be familiar with the Greek word *nikē*, the noun form of *nikaō*, which means "victory." The apostle John uses both words when he writes: "Everyone who is a child of God conquers [*nikaō*] the world. And this is the victory [*nikē*] that conquers [*nikaō*] the world—our faith" (1 John 5:4 NCV).

- Based on how the apostles Paul and John describe the victory that is ours, how would you describe its opposite, *defeat*? In other words, how might we refuse or thwart our victory, perhaps especially when we are suffering?

- Trusting that God is always at work for our good does not mean pretending we don't feel the pain of loss or that everything in life is beautiful when it's not. Jesus never flinched from acknowledging the reality of suffering; instead, he gave us reason to hope in an even deeper reality. We get a glimpse of both reality and deeper reality in the words Jesus spoke to his disciples after preparing them for his own impending death:

I have told you all this so that you may have peace in me. Here on earth you will have many trials and sorrows. But take heart, because I have overcome [*nikaō*] the world (John 16:33 NLT).

If living in victory is possible even in the midst of "many trials and sorrows," how would you describe what that victory is?

In what ways, if any, have you experienced the deeper reality Jesus describes?

5. At the end of the video, Max suggested a simple exercise. Think for a moment about Paul's words: "In everything God works for the good of those who love him" (Romans 8:28 NCV). Remove the word *everything* and replace it with whatever symbolizes a tragedy or hardship in your life. For example, "In hospital stays God works for the good," "In divorce papers God works for the good," "In prison terms God works for the good." How would *you* complete the sentence?

In _____ God works for the good.

Walking Together through Lent

6. Take a few moments to discuss what you've learned and experienced together throughout the *He Chose the Nails* study.

   • In each session, you considered several Easter images and the gifts they represent. Which of these gifts did you find most meaningful or helpful as you walked through Lent? Share the reason for your response.

Session 1: Jesus' crown of thorns as a symbol of Christ's power over sin

Session 2: the nails in Jesus' cross as a symbol of reconciliation with God

Session 3: Jesus' robe and the torn temple curtain as symbols of our access to God's presence

Session 4: Jesus' cross as a symbol of sanctification

Session 5: Jesus' discarded grave clothes as a symbol of Christ's victory over death

- In session 1, you considered how Lent is a season that prepares us to return to God with all our heart. In what ways, if any, did this perspective change how you thought about or experienced Lent this year?

- Overall, how would you describe your experience of the weekly Lenten practices? To what degree, if any, did they help you to prepare spiritually for Easter? What was it like to read the same Scriptures together and then share your watchwords each week?

• How have you recognized God's work among you as a group throughout the study?

INDIVIDUAL ACTIVITY: WHAT I WANT TO REMEMBER (2 MINUTES)

Complete this activity on your own.

1. Briefly review the outline and any notes you took.
2. In the space below, write down the most significant thing you gained in this session—from the teaching, activities, or discussions.

What I want to remember from this session . . .

LENTEN PRACTICE

Before concluding, briefly review the session 5 practice, "Bring It to the Hill." If your group is ongoing, allow time at your next gathering to talk about your experience of the practice. If this is your last group meeting, consider sharing your experience with a friend or another member of the group one-on-one in the coming days.

CLOSING PRAYER

Close your time together with prayer.

Lenten Practice

Listen carefully: Unless a grain of wheat is
buried in the ground, dead to the world, it is
never any more than a grain of wheat. But if
it is buried, it sprouts and reproduces itself
many times over. In the same way, anyone
who holds on to life just as it is destroys that
life. But if you let it go, reckless in your love,
you'll have it forever, real and eternal.
John 12:24–25 MSG

BRING IT TO THE HILL

Just as Jesus died, was buried, and rose again to new life, God's
transforming work in our lives often follows a paschal pattern.
At the close of the group session, Max touched on this idea when

he said we all need to bring something to Calvary, the hill where Christ was crucified.

> In order for the cross of Christ to be the cross of your life, you and I need to bring something to the hill. We have seen what Jesus brought. . . . Now we ask, what will we bring? You can observe the cross and analyze the cross. You can read about it, even pray to it. But until you leave something there, you haven't embraced the cross.[21]

Max suggested starting with our bad moments and mad moments: selfish moods, self-defeating habits (of thought, feeling, or behavior), white lies, misuse of time, angry outbursts, binges, people pleasing, mistakes, substance abuse, bitterness, cheating, mismanaging money, regret, gossip, neglect, bigotries, bad attitudes, pride, or slander. We can also bring our anxious moments to the hill: worries, fears, anxieties, and emotional struggles. Max writes:

> Take your anxieties to the cross—literally. Next time you're worried about your health or house or finances or flights, take a mental trip up the hill. . . . Knowing all he did for you there, don't you think he'll look out for you here?[22]

In addition to continuing daily reflection on Scripture, the invitation in this final week of the study is to embrace the cross—to leave something on the hill each day that you know you need to die to in order to receive new life.

Choose an area of concern to focus on. It might be a specific issue (such as the examples above of bad, mad, and anxious

moments), or a difficult relationship or circumstance. Whenever
the issue or situation arises, ask yourself, *What does letting go—
leaving this at the hill—require of me in this moment?* Take a
timeout to think about it if you need to. Then do it. Allow leaving
it at the hill to determine your demeanor, your body language,
your words, your actions. If you find it helpful, write a reminder
on a Post-it note or create an alert on an electronic device: "Leave
it at the hill."

At the beginning or end of each day this week, set aside
fifteen to twenty minutes to read and prayerfully reflect on the
Daily Scripture Readings (see page 118).

- Begin with a brief time of silence (one to two minutes).

- In God's loving presence, reflect for a few moments on one
  or more of the following questions: *What was I able to
  leave at the hill yesterday? What did I fail to leave at the
  hill yesterday? What do I need to leave at the hill right
  now?*

- Ask the Lord to speak to you through what you are about
  to read. Read the Scripture passages for the day slowly
  and prayerfully, paying attention to anything that sparks
  a connection between the text and your life. This is your
  "watchword" for the day. It might be a promise, a word of
  wisdom, an admonition, a comfort, or an encouragement.

- Read your watchword again, receiving what you read as
  God's words especially for you. Then prayerfully reflect
  on the following questions: *What do I sense God may be
  saying to me? If I were to take these words seriously, how*

would I respond? Spend time in silence again to listen for God, asking him to make his message clear to you.

- Use a journal or the space provided to write down your watchword, your responses to the reflection questions, or any other observations about your experience of reading and listening for God.

- Close your time by asking God to help you trust him with everything you leave at the hill, and to use your watchword to continue speaking to you throughout the day ahead.

- At the end of the week, review your daily reflections and observations. What stands out most to you about what God is saying to you? Write your observations in the space provided or in a journal.

If your group is ongoing, bring your notes to the next group gathering. If your group has concluded, consider sharing your observations and experiences from this week's practice with a friend or another member of the group one-on-one in the coming days.

DAILY SCRIPTURE READINGS

DAY 1

Morning Psalm: *Psalm 118*

Old Testament: *Exodus 3:16–4:12*

Epistle: *Romans 12*

Gospel: *John 8:46–59*

Evening Psalm: *Psalm 145*

DAY 2

Morning Psalm: *Psalm 31*

Old Testament: *Exodus 4*

Epistle: *1 Corinthians 14:1–19*

Gospel: *Mark 9:30–41*

Evening Psalm: *Psalm 35*

DAY 3

Morning Psalm: *Psalms 121–123*

Old Testament: *Exodus 5:1–6:1*

Epistle: *1 Corinthians 14:20–40*

Gospel: *Mark 9:42–50*

Evening Psalm: *Psalms 124–126*

DAY 4

Morning Psalm: *Psalm 119:145–176*

Old Testament: *Exodus 7:8–24*

Epistle: *2 Corinthians 2:14–3:6*

Gospel: *Mark 10:1–16*

Evening Psalm: *Psalms 128–130*

DAY 5

Morning Psalm: *Psalms 131–132*

Old Testament: *Exodus 7:25–8:19*

Epistle: *2 Corinthians 3:7–18*

Gospel: *Mark 10:17–31*

Evening Psalm: *Psalms 140; 142*

DAY 6

Morning Psalm: *Psalms 95; 22*

Old Testament: *Exodus 9:13–35*

Epistle: *2 Corinthians 4:1–12*

Gospel: *Mark 10:32–45*

Evening Psalm: *Psalms 141; 143*

DAY 7

Morning Psalm: *Psalms 137; 144*

Old Testament: *Exodus 10:21–11:8*

Epistle: *2 Corinthians 4:13–18*

Gospel: *Mark 10:46–52*

Evening Psalm: *Psalms 42–43*

Day 1 Reflections and Observations

Day 2 Reflections and Observations

Day 3 Reflections and Observations

Day 4 Reflections and Observations

Day 5 Reflections and Observations

Day 6 Reflections and Observations

Day 7 Reflections and Observations

Week in Review

Briefly review your daily reflections and observations. What stands out most to you about what God is saying to you?

He Chose to Give Us Confidence

Beginning with Moses and all the Prophets,
he explained to them what was said in
all the Scriptures concerning himself.
Luke 24:27

Always, everywhere God is present, and always
he seeks to discover himself to each one.
A. W. Tozer, The Pursuit of God

GROUP DISCUSSION: CHECKING IN (15 MINUTES)

A key part of getting to know God better is sharing your journey with others. Briefly check in with one another about your experiences since the last session. As time permits, discuss one or more of the following questions:

- Briefly share your experience of the session 5 practice, "Bring It to the Hill." The focus of this practice was to embrace the cross by letting go of something you needed to die to in order to receive new life. What kinds of things did letting go—leaving your struggles or anxieties at the cross—require of you this week?

- In what ways, if any, did you receive new life as a result of letting go?

- What was the most meaningful or helpful watchword you identified in your daily Scripture reading? How did God use it to challenge, encourage, or comfort you?

- What similarities or differences do you notice among the watchwords that each person in the group identified this week?

STUDY: *HE CHOSE TO GIVE US CONFIDENCE* (45 MINUTES)

For this week's study, you'll spend extended time exploring the biblical foundation for confidence that Jesus is the Messiah who saves us from sin.

Having Doubts

1. It is human nature to question ideas, try to make sense of our circumstances, and seek to prove that the object of our trust is in fact trustworthy. We want to know that when someone makes a promise to us, we can rely on them to keep it. This was certainly true of the people in the Bible. We find that Abraham and Sarah, Moses, Gideon, and others all wanted to make sure they could trust God's promises. Listed below are Scripture passages that explore how each of these biblical characters wrestled with God's promises. Go around the group and have each person read aloud two or three verses at a time. Then use the questions that follow to continue your discussion.

   • *Abraham and Sarah.* Read Genesis 17:15–22 and 18:10–15. What three words or phrases would you use to describe how Abraham responded to God's promises? How Sarah responded?

- *Moses*. Read Exodus 3:7–14. God promised Moses that he would rescue the Israelites from the Egyptians and that he would be with Moses when Moses spoke to Pharaoh. What stands out most to you about how Moses responded to God's promises?

- *Gideon*. Read Judges 6:11–18. Compare and contrast Gideon's response to God's promises with the responses of Abraham, Sarah, and Moses. How would you describe the similarities and differences?

- Based on these passages, how would you characterize God's response when we have doubts about his promises?

2. As we have seen throughout this study, the greatest promise that God gave to his people is that he would send a Messiah to save them from sin. The Old Testament includes more than 300 prophecies about this promised Savior who would come into the world and restore the relationship between God and humankind. What do the following verses say would happen to the Messiah?

- Psalm 41:9 and Psalm 55:12–14

- Psalm 22:18

- Psalm 22:1

- Psalm 34:19–20

- Zechariah 12:10

- Psalm 16:9–11

3. The Gospels reveal that Jesus is the fulfillment of these Old Testament prophecies. Again and again we read the words "so that Scripture would be fulfilled" in the context of Jesus' last days on earth. Jesus used his final days to offer us proof of who he is and why he came. How do the following verses show that Jesus fulfilled God's promises concerning the Messiah?

- His betrayal: John 18:1–9

- His clothing: John 19:23–24

- He is forsaken by God: Matthew 27:46

- His legs not broken: John 19:36

- His side pierced: John 19:37

- His victory over death: John 20:9

Encountering Christ

4. After Jesus' resurrection, he met two followers on the road
    to Emmaus, a town located about seven miles away from
    Jerusalem. These two men had hoped that Jesus was the
    promised Messiah, but his death brought their dreams—and
    their faith—to a sudden and tragic end. And now there was
    a rumor going around that only added to their pain and con-
    fusion. They said:

> In addition, some of our women amazed us. They
> went to the tomb early this morning but didn't find
> his body. They came and told us that they had seen a
> vision of angels, who said he was alive. Then some of
> our companions went to the tomb and found it just as
> the women had said, but they did not see Jesus (Luke
> 24:22–24).

The two men were overcome with grief and disillusionment in light of the tragic events of the past few days. They
had not yet made the connection between God's promises in
Scripture and Jesus' death on the cross as part of God's plan
to remove sin and restore our relationship with him. They
were confused, doubting, and heartbroken. Listen to Jesus'
reaction:

He said to them, "How foolish you are, and how slow
to believe all that the prophets have spoken! Did not
the Messiah have to suffer these things and then enter his glory?" And beginning with Moses and all the
Prophets, he explained to them what was said in all the
Scriptures concerning himself (Luke 24:25–27).

- Read the full story in Luke 24:13–36. Based on the questions the men asked each other about Jesus as well as
  their countenance and posture, how would you characterize their doubts and disillusionment?

- Consider how Jesus chooses to encounter and interact
  with the two disciples in this story—when he shows
  up, what he says and does not say, and how his presence impacts them. Why do you imagine Jesus refrained
  from revealing who he was right away? What does Jesus'
  approach to these two followers tell you about him? What
  does his approach suggest about how he might choose to
  reveal himself to us today?

- How did the men describe Jesus in verses 19 and 21?
  What does this description tell you about the state of
  their hope in God's promises?

- Looking back on their Emmaus road experience, the two disciples later realized that even before Jesus revealed himself plainly, they recognized him by the impact his words and the truth of Scripture had on their hearts (see verse 32). How did this recognition impact their ability to have confidence in Christ—to trust his promises and to believe that he was who he said he was (see verses 33–35)?

5. The two followers were enthralled! Their doubts were lifted as Jesus opened the Scriptures to them and they began to understand God's greater plan. Note that Jesus started at the beginning "with Moses" and continued with "*all* the Prophets." All of Scripture centers on Jesus, for it is the primary witness that Jesus is who he says he is.

    - In what ways, if any, do you relate to the two men on the road to Emmaus and their journey of faith? What was it that gave you confidence in Christ and helped you to trust his promises?

    - In what small or large ways has the truth of Jesus' resurrection and the gifts of the cross impacted your life recently?

- To what degree does God's faithfulness in the past influence your ability to trust and have confidence that he will keep his promises in the future? A little, a lot, somewhere in between? Share the reasons for your response.

Optional Bible Exploration and Discussion

God's Word contains many more promises for believers in Christ. What do the following verses say to you about what God will do in your life?

- Joshua 1:9

- Psalm 50:15

- Ezekiel 36:26–27

- Malachi 3:10

- Romans 8:1–2

- 1 John 1:9

Walking Together through Lent

6. Take a few moments to reflect on what you've learned in this session.

   - How has reflecting on the proof the Scriptures provide about Jesus impacted your confidence in God's promises?

   - Since you began this study, how has learning more about the magnitude of Jesus' sacrifice on the cross changed the way you relate to Christ or understand who God is?

- It will soon be Easter! In light of your experience of Lent, what are you most looking forward to on Easter Sunday?

CLOSING PRAYER

Close your time together with prayer.

Lenten Practice

He made himself nothing by taking the very
nature of a servant, being made in human
likeness. And being found in appearance
as a man, he humbled himself by becoming
obedient to death—even death on a cross!

Philippians 2:7–8

DAILY SCRIPTURE READINGS FOR HOLY WEEK

Depending on when your study began, your group may or may
not conclude prior to Holy Week. The following readings and
journal pages are provided for those who wish to continue a
practice of daily reading and reflecting on Scripture throughout
Holy Week.

DAILY SCRIPTURE READINGS

DAY 1: PALM SUNDAY
Morning Psalm: *Psalms 24; 29*
Old Testament: *Zechariah 9:9–12*
Epistle: *1 Timothy 6:12–16*
Gospel: *Luke 19:41–48*
Evening Psalm: *Psalm 103*

DAY 2: MONDAY
Morning Psalm: *Psalm 51*
Old Testament: *Lamentations 1:1–12*
Epistle: *2 Corinthians 1:1–7*
Gospel: *Mark 11:12–25*
Evening Psalm: *Psalm 69:1–23*

DAY 3: TUESDAY
Morning Psalm: *Psalms 6; 12*
Old Testament: *Lamentations 1:17–22*
Epistle: *2 Corinthians 1:8–22*
Gospel: *Mark 11:27–33*
Evening Psalm: *Psalm 94*

DAY 4: WEDNESDAY
Morning Psalm: *Psalm 55*
Old Testament: *Lamentations 2:1–17*

Epistle: *2 Corinthians 1:23–2:11*
Gospel: *Mark 12:1–11*
Evening Psalm: *Psalm 74*

DAY 5: MAUNDY THURSDAY
Morning Psalm: *Psalm 102*
Old Testament: *Lamentations 2:10–18*
Epistle: *1 Corinthians 10:14–17; 11:27–32*
Gospel: *Mark 14:12–25*
Evening Psalm: *Psalms 142–143*

DAY 6: GOOD FRIDAY
Morning Psalm: *Psalms 95; 22*
Old Testament: *Lamentations 3:1–9, 19–33*
Epistle: *1 Peter 1:10–20*
Gospel: *John 13:36–38*
Evening Psalm: *Psalms 40; 54*

DAY 7: HOLY SATURDAY
Morning Psalm: *Psalms 137; 144*
Old Testament: *Exodus 10:21–11:8*
Epistle: *2 Corinthians 4:13–18*
Gospel: *Mark 10:46–52*
Evening Psalm: *Psalms 42–43*

Day 1 Reflections and Observations

Day 2 Reflections and Observations

Day 3 Reflections and Observations

Day 4 Reflections and Observations

Day 5 Reflections and Observations

Day 6 Reflections and Observations

Day 7 Reflections and Observations

Week in Review

Briefly review your daily reflections and observations. What stands out most to you about what God is saying to you?

Notes

1. Richard D. Patterson, "Joel," in *The Expositor's Bible Commentary*, Frank E. Gaebelein, gen. ed., vol. 7 (Grand Rapids: Zondervan, 1985), 233.
2. N. T. Wright, *Lent for Everyone: Matthew, Year A* (Louisville: Westminster John Knox Press, 2011), 13.
3. Cornelius Van Dam, *"qr'*," in *New International Dictionary of Old Testament Theology and Exegesis*, Willem A. VanGemeren, gen. ed., vol. 3 (Grand Rapids: Zondervan, 1997), 993.
4. J. A. Thompson and Elmer A. Martens, *"šwb*," in *New International Dictionary of Old Testament Theology and Exegesis*, Willem A. VanGemeren, gen. ed., vol. 4 (Grand Rapids: Zondervan, 1997), 56.
5. M. G. Easton, "Crown," in *Easton's Bible Dictionary* (New York: Scriptura Press, 1893, 2015), 169.
6. C. S. Lewis, *The Great Divorce: A Fantastic Bus Ride from Hell to Heaven—A Round Trip for Some but Not for Others* (New York: Macmillan, 1946), 123.
7. N. T. Wright, *Lent for Everyone*, 2.

8. Hans Bietenhard, "Enemy, Enmity, Hate," in *New International Dictionary of New Testament Theology*, Colin Brown, gen. ed., vol. 1 (Grand Rapids: Zondervan, 1975, 1986), 553.

9. Herwart Vorländer, "Reconciliation," in *New International Dictionary of New Testament Theology*, Colin Brown, gen. ed., vol. 3 (Grand Rapids: Zondervan, 1975, 1986), 168–169.

10. Timothy J. Keller, "More Wicked but More Loved," February 4, 2015, dailykeller.com, accessed April 15, 2016.

11. Eugene H. Peterson, *Tell It Slant: A Conversation on the Language of Jesus in His Stories and Prayers* (Grand Rapids: Wm. B. Eerdmans, 2008), 269.

12. A. W. Tozer, *The Pursuit of God* (Seattle: CreateSpace Independent Publishing, 2014), 23.

13. A. W. Tozer, *Tozer on the Almighty God: A 365-Day Devotional* (Chicago: Moody Publishers, 2004.

14. Paraphrase of W. Harold Mare, "1 Corinthians," in *The Expositor's Bible Commentary*, Frank E. Gaebelein, gen. ed., vol. 10 (Grand Rapids: Zondervan, 1976), 223.

15. Wayne Grudem, *Systematic Theology: An Introduction to Biblical Doctrine* (Grand Rapids: Zondervan, 1994), 746.

16. Dallas Willard, *Renovation of the Heart: Putting On the Character of Christ* (Colorado Springs: NavPress, 2002), 226–227.

17. John Ortberg, *Soul Keeping: Caring for the Most Important Part of You* (Grand Rapids: Zondervan, 2014), 122.

18. Dallas Willard, *Renovation of the Heart*, 227.

19. Donald K. McKim, "paschal mystery," "paschal lamb," in *The Westminster Dictionary of Theological Terms*, Second

Edition (Louisville: Westminster John Knox Press, 2014), 229.

20. Eugene H. Peterson, *A Long Obedience in the Same Direction: Discipleship in an Instant Society*, Revised and Expanded Edition (Downers Grove, Ill.: InterVarsity Press, 1980, 2000), 100.

21. Max Lucado, *He Chose the Nails: What God Did to Win Your Heart* (Nashville: Thomas Nelson, 2000), 139–140.

22. Ibid., 140.

Also available by Max Lucado

He Chose the Nails

$\mathcal{W}$ ith his warm, caring style, Max examines the symbols surrounding Christ's crucifixion, revealing the claims of the cross and asserting that if they are true, then Christianity itself is true. The supporting evidence either makes the cross the single biggest hoax of all time, or the hope of all humanity.